Investing in Real Estate

How to Get into the Real Estate Game with NO MONEY DOWN

© **Copyright 2017 by** _____ **- All rights reserved.**

The following eBook is reproduced below with the goal of providing information that is as accurate and reliable as possible. Regardless, purchasing this eBook can be seen as consent to the fact that both the publisher and the author of this book are in no way experts on the topics discussed within and that any recommendations or suggestions that are made herein are for entertainment purposes only. Professionals should be consulted as needed prior to undertaking any of the action endorsed herein.

This declaration is deemed fair and valid by both the American Bar Association and the Committee of Publishers Association and is legally binding throughout the United States.

Furthermore, the transmission, duplication or reproduction of any of the following work including specific information will be considered an illegal act irrespective of if it is done electronically or in print. This extends to creating a secondary or tertiary copy of the work or a recorded copy and is only allowed with the express written consent of the Publisher. All additional rights are reserved.

The information in the following pages is broadly considered to be a truthful and accurate account of facts and as such any inattention, use or misuse of the information in question by the reader will render any resulting actions solely under their purview. There are no scenarios in which the publisher or the original author of this work can be in any fashion deemed liable for any hardship or damages that may befall them after undertaking information described herein.

Additionally, the information in the following pages is intended only for informational purposes and should thus be thought of as universal. As befitting its nature, it is presented without assurance regarding its prolonged validity or interim quality. Trademarks that are mentioned are done without written consent and can in no way be considered an endorsement from the trademark holder.

Table of Contents

Introduction 1

Chapter 1: Maximize Your Borrowing Position 3

Chapter 2: Finding the Right Property 13

Chapter 3: Nontraditional Loans 24

Chapter 4: Property Wholesaling 34

Chapter 5: Fix and Flip 44

Chapter 6: Rent to Own Rental Properties 54

Conclusion 63

Introduction

Congratulations on downloading *Investing in Real Estate: How to Get into the Real Estate Game with NO MONEY DOWN* and thank you for doing so. Real estate investment is one of the oldest means of investment imaginable, having been around since slightly after the concept of property ownership itself and it is easy to see why. With a few notable exceptions, the market will always slowly and surely improve because as everyone knows, they aren't making any more land. While almost everyone understands the benefit of this type of investment, many people end their thoughts on it there as they feel as though they will never be able to afford to make this type of investment.

It is this inaccurate mindset that keeps many people from achieving the type of prosperity that real estate investing affords, and it could not be further from the truth. In fact, there are a wide variety of different ways to start making money from the real estate investment game, and they will be discussed in-depth in the following chapters. First, you will learn all about making yourself look as attractive to lenders as possible by maximizing your borrowing position. You will then learn all about finding the right type of property to generate the type of deal a lender can't help but say yes to.

Then you will learn all about the different types of nontraditional loans you will need to consider when it comes to getting started in real estate investment for no money down. From there you will learn about the ease and benefits of property wholesaling, how to ensure you turn a profit from entering into a fix and flip scenario, and how to turn rent to own properties into rental properties without paying a dime.

There are plenty of books on this subject on the market, thanks again for choosing this one! Every effort was made to ensure it is full of as much useful information as possible, please enjoy!

Chapter 1: Maximize Your Borrowing Position

Buying an investment property with no money down is a difficult task, no two ways about it. Difficult doesn't mean impossible, however, which is why you will need to be willing to work twice as hard for less reward than those who are able to purchase property in a more traditional fashion. Less doesn't mean insubstantial, however, and if you start out willing to take what you can get when it comes to returns on no-money-down investments, and you save your profits, you will soon find that you can afford to make a more profitable investment all on your own.

When it comes to borrowing money to pay for an investment property, the only way a traditional lender is going to lend you the money to finance a home loan with no money down is if you have so much collateral that it is unlikely you wouldn't be able to come to a more manageable agreement. This means you are going to need to look at private lenders, hard money lenders and crowdfunding options to generate the capital you are looking for. Contrary to popular belief, this means you are going to need to have all of your ducks more in a row, not less. If you are coming at a lender with nothing but your hat in hand and a great idea then you are going to need to do everything in your power in order to maximize your borrower position. In order to go about doing so, consider the following tips.

General rules for borrower strength

Tools at your disposal: In order to ensure that you get the best possible rate on any loan that you do manage to find, it is important that you understand just what tools you have at your disposal. First things first, you are going to need to ensure that you have a credit score of as close to 700 as possible. While non-traditional lenders are willing to work with clients with less than stellar credit ratings, the better your credit score is the better your rates will ultimately be. The Great Recession proved that a good credit score isn't all that is needed to ensure a reliable return on an investment of this magnitude so you are also going to be at an advantage your first time as you don't have any previous investment experience or a lengthy credit history. Again, this doesn't mean it is impossible, it just means that when you approach potential lenders you will need to be prepared to go through the wringer.

While this is something you are clearly trying to avoid, it is important to understand that for a traditional loan the average financial institution will give out a loan for about 80 percent of the ARV price of a property and a hard money lender will give out just 60 percent. As someone who is trying to avoid putting this money down, your job is then going to be coming up with a way to prove that your investment is worth throwing in that extra money as well. While financial institutions won't be able to help you, hard money lenders and a few other options discussed in the next chapter should still conceivably be able to help you out.

If the only thing standing between you and a traditional loan is that 20 percent and you are looking for a reasonably priced property, then you may instead be able to qualify for multiple smaller loans that don't require down payments and then take the profits and pay them off as quickly as possible. The interest from an additional loan is going to severely skew the profit margins that you may have previously come up with and more than that will completely leave them in shambles. If you consider going down this route then you need to be extremely confident in your ability to find a deal as the cost of failure for this course of action is exceedingly high.

Credit score: When it comes to credit it is equally important to know your credit score as anything less than 740 for a traditional financial institution and 700 for a private money lender is going to result in you paying more in interest than you otherwise would. In general, you can realistically expect to see rates that are 2 points higher for every 10 points below these numbers that your score is currently at.

Personal details: Furthermore, it is important that you prepare yourself prior to reaching out to any lenders with a full list of all of your expenses along with your current investment portfolio. You will need to show a steady source of income for the past 6 months (the higher the better) and will also need to ensure that you can support yourself and pay all of your bills for 3 months, while still making the designated loan payments. These are standard requirements for most loans, though what you are required to provide for a complete loan is likely to be much more involved.

When it comes to talking to potential lenders, it is important to understand that you are looking to build a long-term relationship with this person which means you need to consider more than if they are going to give you all the money that you are asking for. You will ideally be looking for someone that is looking to build a mutually beneficial relationship within the long-term, which will help to ensure that the rates you see from the experience will improve over time as well. Additionally, with a lender partnership, you will be able to generate strategies in the long-term that are more likely to benefit every in the long run. You will need to stay away from real estate brokers no matter what, however, as they are going to be looking to place limitations on the types of properties that you are able to purchase, potentially hurting your profits in the process.

In order to find a lender that is going to help facilitate your long-term goals, it is important to be picky, and not just go with the first one that is willing to facilitate your loan. You are going to want to interview them, just as much as they are interviewing you and ascertain the number of investors they are working with, the number of loans they would allow you to have at a time (you never know when a second deal will come along) and the types of real estate investments they are most likely to provide loans for.

These questions and others like them will make it easier for you to determine if you and the lender will ultimately be on the same page when it comes to the future, not based on a simple sales pitch but rather based on the true facts of the situations. What's more, knowing what they are looking for will help you to know how to alter your pitch before you give it in order to ensure the best possible results. Finally, if you don't like the answers you receive it is important to not be so worried about not getting the money that you make the wrong decision. If you move on you will find a better solution somewhere else, and even if your initial deal falls through, it can still be taken to other lenders as a proof of concept for what you are capable of that can help to speed up the process the next time around.

Consider your available credit: First and foremost, just because you are looking into nontraditional types of loans doesn't mean that the traditional paradigms don't apply. This means, first and foremost that you will want to ensure your total available credit (the maximum that you can charge to all of your credit cards) is at least twice the amount of what you currently owe on said credit cards. The smaller the number in this situation the better as it represents your credit card utilization rate.

While it is beneficial to have a low credit utilization rate, the difference between the numbers above, when you are applying for a loan with the hope of securing zero money down, it is even more beneficial to have as few credit cards as possible. Lenders in these situations see each credit card as a potential well for a new debt which could take priority over the debt that you owe to them. For example, if you have a total of 4 credit cards, with a total balance of $2,000 and a total limit of $45,000, then that is $43,000 worth of potential debt that is ready and waiting to strike.

This can be a tricky situation if you aren't in a position to immediately pay off what you owe in order to ensure you credit utilization remains intact as possible while still canceling credit cards. The best way to go about doing so is to consolidate the debt as much as possible onto the card with the best rates, then, right before you start looking for lenders, cancel your other cards. The fact that your credit utilization rate has changed won't reach your credit reports for months, as the process for updating such things is woefully out of date. It is even entirely possible that the change won't be noticed for years, if at all. Finally, if it is noticed, credit utilization isn't nearly as important to your overall credit score as some other factors so if you are good in general then you should still be fine.

Once you have canceled the cards then you will be free to approach lenders with an available credit card balance that is much less scary while still receiving the benefits when it comes to your credit rating which they will also be checking. If the search for a lender ends up taking too long you can then request to renew your card, which should speed you through the process of reapplying normally, and repeat as needed.

Clean credit history: One of the best ways to ensure that lenders of all shapes and sizes are willing to work with you is to ensure that your credit history is as clean as it can possibly be. While day to day this means paying your bills on time and ensuring that any issues you have with creditors are cleared up before things get serious, there are also a few things you can do to clear up past blemishes if you haven't been as vigilant at keeping your credit score clean as you should have been.

The first step to clearing up past mistakes is to get a copy of all three of your credit reports which are available for free thanks to the Fair Credit Report Act. You can order your free reports from AnnualCreditReport.com. When you receive it, you are going to want to take note of every negative item that you can find, as well as the details relating to where it came from and from how long ago it was. If there is anything on the report that is more than 7 years old, all you need to do is write a letter to the credit bureau and alert them to the fact and they will fix things up for you.

Regardless of what the issue is, however, you can use the fact that the laws regarding credit reporting were written before the invention of the internet which means there are loopholes that you can work around. First things first, you are going to want to write a letter to the bureaus disputing the issues that you are experiencing. It doesn't matter if the issue is legitimate or not, if they can't find proof to back it up right away then it will be dismissed.

For the issues that they have proof of, this is still not the end, all you have to do is not give an inch when it comes to the issue. The next step will be to report back to the them that the information is still not correct and that you are requesting a verification of their files as allowed by Section 609 of the FCRA. You will likely receive several letters in response that are trying to scare you, but the truth of the matter is that Section 609 requires a paper copy of the documents in question and the bureaus have been accepting digital reports from lenders for nearly 20 years.

To ensure that you will always get a response, you will need to include a copy of your photo ID in the letter, along with a copy of your social security card. These are crucial as failing to do so will result in your letter being thrown out as technical they only have to answer letters from people whose identification is verified. Yes, it is ridiculous, but if you are going to play by the rules, so will they. Send out the following letter and keep sending it once a month until they tell you what you want to hear.

Name

Address

(Credit Bureau Name)

Date

To Whom It May Concern:

This letter is a formal complaint that you are reporting inaccurate and incomplete credit information. I am distressed that you have included the below information in my credit profile and have failed to maintain reasonable procedures in your operations to assure maximum possible accuracy in the credit reports you publish.

Credit reporting laws ensure that bureaus report only 100% accurate credit information. Every step must be taken to assure the information reported is completely accurate and correct. The following information, therefore, needs to be re-investigated. I respectfully request to be provided proof that these inquiries were in fact authorized with an instrument bearing my signature, and for legitimate business purposes. Failing that, the unauthorized inquiry must be deleted from the report as soon as possible:

(Accounts you wish to have removed from your report)

Please delete this misleading information, and supply a corrected credit profile to all creditors who have received a copy within the last 6 months, or the last 2 years for employment purposes.

Additionally, please provide the name, address, and telephone number of each credit grantor or another subscriber.

Under federal law, you have 30 days to complete your re-investigation. Be advised that the description of the procedure used to determine the accuracy and completeness of the information is hereby requested as well, to be provided within 15 days of the completion of your re-investigation.

Sincerely,

(Signature)

Name

SSN#

Chapter 2: Finding the Right Property

If you ever hope to be able to purchase a property for absolutely no money down then the first thing you are going to need is to have a potential property in mind that is priced as cheaply as possible. The truth of the matter is that finding a house that can turn a profit is easy, finding a house that can turn a profit with none of your own money down can take a lot of work.

If you ever hope to find the best deals then the first thing you are going to need to understand is that you are going to be dealing with a much smaller overall pool of properties which means it is going to take much more diligence and hard work in order to hit pay dirt. You are also going to need to consider a wide variety of properties at all times as it is much more likely for these types of properties to fizzle out prior to completion.

MLS: If you hope to find properties that are truly underpriced then the first place that you are going to want to look is the first place that everyone else looks the Multiple Listing Service. The MLS is the repository of all the properties nationwide that are currently for sale through a licensed real estate agent. As this is the primary destination for those who are thinking about buying a house, the competition is naturally going to be exceedingly fierce. This doesn't mean that it isn't possible to find a great deal however, you just need to be willing to work for it.

Initially, this means you are going to want to check the listings first thing in the morning, as in 4 am EST and again at about 9 pm PST. Furthermore, you are going to want to ensure that you pay special attention to any property that is listed on a Friday as they are always going to have less competition because some folks are always anxious to start the weekend early. Furthermore, it is important to remain consistent when it comes to listings that are difficult to get a hold of as if you are having a hard time contacting someone, odds are everyone else is as well. Being persistent can often pay huge dividends as the person likely feels as though the interest in the property is low which will only ever work out in your favor. Perseverance is key to the success you are looking for.

While you never know when a good deal might materialize, one thing you can know for certain is the fact that when it does it won't last long. As such, you need to be able to act on any MLS deal that you come across as soon as possible. Depending on your funding plan, you might not be able to do anything practical with the first great deal you find. However, you can then use that great deal as the basis for a pitch to a hard money lender who then might be so impressed that they pre-approve you for the next property you find which is when you can get out, see property and be ready to make the kind of deals you need to make in order to find the success you are looking for.

Once you are ready to move on a deal you have found, it is important to contact the listing agent as soon as possible, when you speak with them you will need to ensure you can drop everything and view the property at their earliest convenience. In this situation, flexibility is key, every hour you wait is another hour that the property can be ripped from your fingertips. Additionally, when you visit the property it is important that you know what types of serious issues to look for, or know how to get in contact with someone who does. Scheduling the second showing is only going to slow down the process and if you have to do so then you can likely kiss the property goodbye. When you leave, you need to be either mentally writing it off or offering to write a check. Any middle ground is just going to end up costing you money.

This means you will need to be willing to make an offer on the spot and follow up on it after it has been accepted. This means you are going to need to be able to accurately determine the after-repair value from the information you have found via the walkthrough or what you managed to research before the meeting. If your ARV assessment skills aren't where they need to be then you will need to practice with other walkthroughs until you are sure of your skills. Finally, when it comes to getting the absolute best possible deal then you are going to want to search out listings that have just gone onto the market for a second time. No one is ever more willing to make a deal than a property owner who just had a deal fall through at the absolute last minute.

Other methods: When it comes to finding undervalued properties in a specific area then you will often find success when you learn to think outside the box. One of the best ways of doing so when it comes to finding a cheap property is to find a potential seller who hasn't yet gotten around to finding a real estate agent. If you can get to the seller before this occurs you will find that they are often much more malleable when it comes to the price, especially when there are secondary considerations in play as well.

In order to find these types of sellers, the first thing that you are going to want to do is take a drive around the areas you are considering buying in. While doing so, you are going to need to be on the lookout for signs that a property owner is likely to be selling sooner than later. Easy ways to make these types of determinations include things like a completion of long-neglected maintenance, packing, and house painting. While you might not notice much at first, a few trips through the neighborhood should be enough to give you an idea of what you are going to be looking for.

While you are out and about you are also going to want to take note of properties that appear vacant and then don't change noticeably in a few months or more. When you find these types of properties, be sure to take note of the address as you can easily find the details for the owner from your local county recorder's office. With this information in hand, reaching out to the owner is as simple as sending a letter explaining that you have seen the property sitting and falling into disrepair and making it clear that you would be interested in making a potentially mutually beneficial deal. While oftentimes you won't hear back, sometimes you will hit upon a property owner who doesn't have the time, resources or energy to deal with the property properly which means the potential for profit is quite high.

Other useful homeowners are those who are currently going through a bit of a rough patch. Essentially, what this means is that you are going to want to do everything in your power in order to find the type of sellers that could generously be called motivated. These types of sellers will be folks with serious debts that need to be cleared up sooner than later and who are the most likely to be inviting a mysterious stranger who shows up on their doorstep with a suitcase full of cash.

The first step in this process is going to be searching online for lists of debt that are being sold in your area. This is actually an extremely common practice and if you are in even a mid-sized city then you should have no problem tracking down what you need. The going rate for those with enough debt to warrant selling a home over is around $250 for about 1,000 names, plenty for your purposes, especially if you are just starting out. If you can't find any lists of debtors in your area then you can instead look up local public records for those in your area who have just been hit with serious fines. This will likely take a bit longer to find success with, but you will ultimately end up with the same list of people who are in a tough financial spot in the moment.

With the list in hand, you are then going to want to cross reference the names with the county recorder's office property ownership records. Each time you find a potential seller, write down their details, the more the merrier as your overall return percentage is going to be quite small at the best of times. When it comes to reaching out to your list, you are going to want to generate a form letter that expresses how sorry you are that they have ended up in their current situation and let them know that you have a way to turn things all around.

Depending on what you feel is a reasonable starting debt amount, you can easily fill in the blanks and offer 30 percent less than market value if not more. You won't want to include this detail in the letter, however, and instead simply mention that you would like to discuss the offer in person if possible. This will let you see the person face to face and get a better read on what sort of deal they may be amenable too. As these individuals are going to be completely unprepared to sell, you will often find them much more willing to deal, especially if you should up to the meeting with a large amount of cash in hand.

In general, with this type of direct mailing campaign, you can often expect anywhere between 1.5 and 3 percent return out of all of the letters you send. This means that if you purchase 1,000 names then you will see up to 30 potential responses which should be plenty to secure your first below-cost property.

High-risk options: When it comes to finding properties on the cheap, there is absolutely no better way of going about doing so than by visiting a property auction. In general, this is done as part of the foreclosure process, or in some cases to pay off other substantial forms of debt. These properties have often been in the system for quite some time which means the previous owners had all the time they needed in order to take out all of their anger on the property itself. While you may be able to arrange to see certain properties beforehand, this is the exception, not the rule which means that you can easily find yourself in the hole for more than the property is worth if you take a gamble and do so poorly. If you aren't willing to take a risk in hopes of a great deal, or you don't know a renovation team that will work on spec then this type of property deal is likely not going to be for you.

While they don't take place in all regions, once a lien holder forecloses on a particular property and the foreclosure has run its course, the last step is what is known as a courthouse step auction, though the actual location may vary. Details regarding these types of actions can often be found online at the local municipality website or in the local paper. The bidding generally starts with what was still owed on the property so it can be extremely lucrative if you can get a decent read on the property before having to commit to the purchase.

These particulars are going to vary from sale to sale, if you can track down details regarding the specifics of the property beforehand then you can likely mitigate a large part of the potential for risk. Greater risk leads to a greater potential for reward, however, and this type of sale can frequently lead to the ownership of properties that you could otherwise never be able to afford given your current budget. If you come across a price that is absolutely too good to pass up, be aware that you are going to need to have a preapproved loan ready and waiting or cash on hand as the sale won't wait for you to take care of these sorts of things after the fact.

Buying foreclosures

While most first-time investors are recommended to shy away from foreclosures because they are easy to get caught up in without first gathering all of the pertinent information and make poor decisions as a result. If you are looking for rock-bottom prices, and you take the time to make sure that you really know what you are doing, then you are just as likely to come out with a winner rather than an accidental lemon. While looking to invest in a property that is in foreclosure, you will typically have three primary points where you can jump in and pick the property up for under market value.

An ideal time to pick up a property during the foreclosure process is once it is clear that foreclosure is the only realistic option but before any formal deals have been made and any resulting rage is then taken out on the property. The price that you find in these types of scenarios is going to be higher than what you would pay for a property during a courthouse step sale but you will be able to do all the research you need in order to ensure the property is up to snuff and also save on potential remodeling fees so it is definitely a course of action to consider.

To locate properties that are in this state the first thing you are going to want to do is to find notices of default filed in the court by major lienholders in your state. These can be found at either your local public records office or with the clerk of the court depending on the size of your city or town. Not all of the loan details you will come across will be relevant, but it is still going to be a good place to look for leads.

When you do track down the relevant soon-to-be former owners, you will often find them extremely eager to negotiate as this is their last chance to get anything out of the property before the bank takes control and they get nothing. It goes without saying that you are going to need to be ready with an offer assuming you check out the property and it is in good condition. A promise to pay in the future won't do these people any good.

If the property doesn't sell at auction, it will then be listed in a traditional fashion, often at slightly more than what you would have paid for it during the auction, though typically still well below market value. When you are looking for properties that are listed as foreclosed or REO in the real estate listing, all of the rules for dealing with the MLS applies. It is important to go into these situations with a clear idea as to what the property is worth and ensure you have someone who can tell you what types of repairs will be required in order to sell to ensure it is worth your while.

Timing is everything

It doesn't matter what type of property you are pursuing when getting the best prices on real estate deals you are either going to want to approach the seller early or very late. In general, if the property owner is in something of a bad way they are going to take the first profitable offer that they come across, assuming it is not currently a seller's market. While some situations will alter this fact, you always need to assume that this is the case with every potential deal you come across. This means that in order to find the truly amazing deals you will need to ensure that you are always looking for the next great deal to ensure that you are in the right place at the right time more often than not.

The most reliable way of putting yourself ahead of the pack is to ensure that you always set out with a clear plan in mind when it comes to what you can afford to pay in order to turn a profit. You will only ever want to deviate from it if you see the unexpected for greater profits in the long-term by doing so. Moving forward with this type of plan will make it easier for you to pounce on premium deals with machine-like precision, rather than letting your emotions get between you and a good deal. Keep in mind that if you end up walking away from a deal to think about it the only thing you are doing is giving other investors the opportunity to swoop in and take your great deal away from you.

Alternately, you may have better luck when it comes to scooping up properties that other people don't especially seem interested in. If you come across listings that are more than 30 days old then you can expect the owner to be worn out and just ready to be done with the entire process. Obviously, this means good news for you and your bottom line as people in this type of emotional state are in no way fit to negotiate for their best interests. You will often find that you can pick these properties up for as much as 15 percent under asking price, more if it is a buyer's market. While these types of properties are often going to require more renovation than some others you will come across, the difference in price will typically still make it worth it.

Chapter 3: Nontraditional Loans

As previously mentioned, getting a traditional mortgage is likely off the table if you are looking to put no money down, but there are still plenty of other options available including private lenders, hard money lenders, owner financing, investors and crowdfunding options.

Hard money lenders: If you don't have the funds to qualify for the down payment on a traditional loan, but are still in generally good shape overall, then a hard money loan might be a viable option. While the interest rate that you have to pay might be somewhat higher, especially on a 100 percent loan, not having the entanglements that come along with some of the other options listed here makes it a viable choice in a lot of situations. What's more, unlike a traditional loan that can take 3 months or more to clear, the average hard money loan can be approved in as little as a week or less. Hard money loans are provided by private professional investors and will be for shorter time periods than traditional loans with a majority of the payments made going towards interest rather than principal.

Hard money lenders are also particularly useful in that they are likely to be more interested in the potential quality of the deal you bring them, including things like supply discounts and contractor teams, than they are about your relative inexperience. While you might not be able to secure the loan you are looking for with your first try, if the deal was solid it should be enough to put you on the lender's radar and get them to elaborate on what you would need to do in order to get a 100 percent loan from them. When it comes to finding these individuals, the best way to do so continues to be the real estate investment club, especially when it comes to those who are open to your unique set of circumstances.

When looking for the right hard money lender you are going to want to keep in mind that they will typically specialize in a single type of real estate investment deal which means that you will need to try a few before you find one who is willing to go with the type of offer you are suggesting. Furthermore, you will also need to keep in mind that they typically operate via what is known as a first lien position which means they will be paid out first once the property is sold, regardless of what the conditions for that sale end up being. You may be able to find a hard money lender who is willing to take a second lien position under certain conditions, but this is something you will certainly sacrifice if you are looking for a 100 percent loan.

While the amount that you are going to ultimately end up paying is certainly going to vary based on where you are looking for the loan and the number of hard money lenders operating in your area, the standard rate is between 10 and 15 percent, though on a 100 percent loan you are more likely looking at anywhere from 25 to 30 percent instead. This is certainly high, and in any other situation, it would be outrageously so, given the circumstances you should be thankful that you found the lender you did and take the rate they offer as you will generally have zero leverage in this situation.

With that in mind, if your finances are in excellent shape and you have the savings to support yourself and the loan for a reasonable period of time, then you will likely still see lower rates than if your specifics are not on point. In fact, you could see up to a 5 percent off the total amount you will need to pay back if you are a picture-perfect candidate. In addition to the interest on your loan, the hard money lender is also going to ask for a portion of the profits in return for putting up all of the capital, regardless of what else besides money you do plan on bringing to the table. The amount they ask for is going to vary based on a variety of factors including the strength of the loan in question but it is always going to be at least 20 percent.

To ensure that your approach to your hard money lender goes successfully, it is crucial that you do so with an airtight plan in hand when it comes to profiting from the property in question. Furthermore, you will need to ensure that your credit score is greater than 600 and that your income to debt ratio is lower than 45 percent. You will also need to ensure that your credit score is free of foreclosures and bankruptcies for at least the previous 10 years. You will also need to show proof that you can afford a full 6 months of your expenses along with the costs of loan repayment for that period of time as well. Finally, you will need to have some type of equity that you can put into the property in lieu of cash to help make them feel more confident in the loan than they otherwise would be.

Crowdfunding options: While it might sound surprising, there are actually several different platforms out there when it comes to crowdfunding a real estate investment loan. In addition to having fewer requirements than other types of loan, these loans can be fully funded in less than 24-hours assuming you have a plan that really blows people away. This means, if you happen to come across a great potential deal without having your infrastructure fully in place, this might be your best chance to come up with the money in a short enough timeframe that you can actually take advantage of it.

Each crowdfunding loan website is going to have slightly different requirements when it comes to just what is required to qualify for a loan. As a good place to start, however, you will need to have a credit score that is higher than 580, a debt ratio that is less than 50 percent and a credit history that is free of foreclosures, short sales, and bankruptcies.

These websites allow any investor to post the details of the property they are looking at, as well as their plan for it, any qualifications they have in the field and any other relevant details before opening the investment process to anyone for any amount they are interested in investing. Investors will then receive a rate of return that you set, proportionate to the amount that they invested in the loan. Rates for these types of loans tend to vary, with rates of around 18 percent being the average though, again, rates for a 100 percent loan are going to be higher due to the additional amount of risk involved.

If you have found a top-notch property and have an excellent credit history along with great credentials, then you are going to want to check out RealtyShares.com. Investors are all accredited which means they are able to invest larger amounts of capital more easily, and the marketplace Is full of pre-screened properties so investors know that the properties that make it onto the site are worth seriously considering.

Another platform that is worth considering is iFunding.com which also offers a wide range of residential projects and a minimum investment of $5,000. The platform is unique, however, in that it also allows those looking for loans to connect with professionals who can more easily list, approve and generate capital for the deal outside of the platform through a wide variety of means.

If your plan is feasible, but you or it isn't quite as airtight as some investors might like, then you may instead want to check out PatchofLand.com which is a peer-to-peer lending platform. The requirements for using the service are much less strict than the other options and investors can invest as much or as little into a project as they like. In fact, the website's stated goal is to become a consistent source of funding for rehabbing properties across the US.

Owner financing: Depending on how you plan on making a profit from the property, you may find that asking the seller for owner financing can be a reliable way to ensure that you don't need to worry about a loan at all, as long as you can get rid of the property before the inspection window closes and you actually need to come up with the money. Prior to 2009, practically anyone could get an investment property loan as long as they were able to actually walk into a bank and ask about receiving one. As such, those who couldn't a loan via traditional means was naturally mistrusted which meant asking about owner financing was a no go.

Things are different these days, however, as it is public knowledge that banks are more skittish when it comes to giving out loans and sellers are more willing to just get anything done regardless of how the deal gets made. In fact, currently, more than 30 percent of all sellers are willing to consider owner financing for the right buyer which means you are going to need to have everything prepared from the previous chapter in order to show that you are a reliable investment. Once you do obtain owner financing you will then sign a promissory note saying when you will pay back the loan in full, what your monthly payments are going to be, when these payments start and what the interest rate is like.

If you have access to a contractor who can get materials on credit, then it is possible that you could sell the owners on the idea of selling you the house with the promise to pay them in full once it is renovated and resold for more than it is going for now. This will obviously not be feasible in all situations, but for owners who are already fairly well off who are not selling for emergency reasons this can be thought of as a type of investment and if you can prove them numbers you might be on to something. In this case, you and the owner would then essentially become partners in the business, and any contracts would need to reflect the way in which the profits are going to be split.

Private lenders: A private money lender is a private citizen that loans out money as a means of investment, typically secured via a note as well as a deed of trust, for the purpose of facilitating a real estate transaction. Private money lenders are often much more relationship-based when compared to hard money lenders. When it comes to determining who is approachable for these type of potential loans, you are going to want to think in terms of social circles.

The first private money lender circle is the primary circle and consists of your friends and family. This should be your initial stop when it comes to looking to raise capital for an investment for obvious reasons; it is easy to find face to face time with these people and they will theoretically be more inclined to say yes to you. This is not always going to be a good thing, however, as it is unlikely that they will know a good deal from the bad which can hurt more than help for your first real estate investment. If you go down this route it is important to make it clear that there is a potential for loss to avoid damaging core relationships down the line.

For a majority of people, these resources are going to be somewhat limited, though it is possible that you might be able to use this circle to generate the capital required for the down payment on the property which could then provide you the time needed to find other funding options. This, in turn, will make your investment appear even more valuable when you put it in front of other types of private lenders.

The secondary private lender circle is going to be comprised of relevant associates of your primary circle that might be inclined to invest in these sorts of things if the deal is right. The more people you know directly, the more secondary contacts you will have as well so a hearty round of networking prior to starting to actively fundraise can lead to improved results. As you have been recommended to this group, they are still likely to be more inclined to what it is you are trying to do than someone you met off the street, though they will only move forward if the deal is actually sound which makes them a valuable sounding board regardless if they invest in you or not.

This circle is also a worthwhile place to spend time seeking funding in as it is likely to represent a much larger pool of potential capital than your primary circle which means it is a good place to look once you already have the deal locked up and are just looking for the funds to capitalize on what you have found. What's more, as these people also likely know each other, at least socially, then it is possible that you can create a group mentality scenario, where initial investments lead to the second round of further investment. The downside to working with this group is that it is likely to take more time to generate the capital required from these relationships, often in proportion to how far you are removed socially from the investor in question. In order to be successful with this group you need to set time aside for plenty of investment presentations and investor luncheons, the more appealing you can make the investment sound, the more likely you are to get the ball rolling.

Finally, the last circle is going to be made up of both accredited investors as well as other investors that were met through traditional advertising efforts. This group is going to have the biggest pool of potential capital of the lot but the investors aren't going to know you personally in any way shape or form which means that they are going to need the most work on your part when it comes to reeling them in.

The easiest way to locate these types of investors are through popular investor websites such as LendPost, Go Big Network, Prosper Marketplace, Lending Club and the BiggerPockets. When posting your investment idea onto these sites it is important that you always work through official channels for your own safety as well as to ensure that you remain within the confines of the SEC laws. Alternately, depending on the amount of time you have available, you may also find success via an investor direct mailing list which can be purchased from sites such as Click2Mail and Melissa Data. These sites will send you mailing details for a wide variety of accredited investors and you then write a mass pitch and send it out in hopes of getting bites. The results for this type of approach can reach as high as 5 percent assuming your pitch is worthwhile.

Chapter 4: Property Wholesaling

When it comes to reliably making money off a real estate investment with no money out of pocket, the simplest way to go about doing so is through the magic of property wholesaling. With this method of real estate investment, you take your time looking for the perfect property, one you can get for a price that is low enough for you to add a margin between what you can buy it for and what you can sell it to another investor for and ensure that it is still a profitable offer. Once you find this type of property, all you are going to be required to do is to get the deal in writing and then sign it over to the second real estate investor in exchange for a finder's fee in short order so you are required to put any money down.

In addition to not requiring you to actually have the money in hand to purchase the property in question, property wholesaling is great because it allows you to avoid all the headaches involved in renovations, and either selling or renting the property out. Research and the right connections are all you are going to need in this scenario in order to turn a reliable profit.

Before you head out and start looking for properties to wholesale, however, the first thing you are going to need to do is to look up the laws in your area when it comes to property wholesaling as they can vary dramatically from place to place. Depending on the laws in your state, property wholesaling will likely be viewed as one of the several different types of transactions, so beneficial to your cause, others, not so much. For example, certain states view it as a purely real estate transaction which means that it can only be completed by someone with a real estate license.

Depending on the deal that you were able to orchestrate with the property owner, it might be worth it to pass the actual deal off to an agreeable real estate agent, or you may want to go ahead and get your real estate license if you plan on making this a regular hobby. Alternately, some states will still allow what is known as a double close which means that you close on the purchase of the property and then wait a few days before closing on the sale of the property. Regardless of how you choose to proceed, it is important that you research laws in your state thoroughly as fines could easily cut steeply into your profits.

When it comes to finding the right people to deal with in order to ensure that you can turn the property around as quickly as possible, the first place you are always going to want to look is your local real estate investment club. While your first pitch might not be met with much enthusiasm, if you follow the process correctly and ensure your numbers are on point, you will almost always be able to find someone who is willing to bite on a good deal. What's more, with your first successful wholesale property under your belt, you will then become a verified good deal and you will likely have many more interested parties the next time you come across the right type of deal.

The people you meet are likely going to be what are known as cash buyers. As the name implies, these individuals are going to be able to put down the cash required to purchase a property ASAP, this might not always be their cash as they might just have access to a reliable hard money or private money lender. Nevertheless, the point is that these types of folks don't need to go through the lengthy loan approval process and can thus help you jump on your good deal before someone else does. These types of real estate investors are always looking for a good deal, you just need to bring it to them.

If you strike out with the real estate investment club, you might have luck finding cash buyers by talking to local real estate agents. While they might not know anyone who fits the bill personally, they can usually give you a list of all of the properties in a given area that were made via a cash sale as this data should be readily available in most cases. With this data in hand, all it will take is a simple public-records search to determine who purchased these homes. While the first person you contact might not be the person with the money, with a little persuasion they can pass you up the line. While not every other investor may be willing to give up their cash money source, doing so doesn't really hurt them in any way so a little perseverance will surely pay off.

While getting to your cash buyer might take a little work, the payoff is sure to be worth it. Cash buyers don't care about how experienced you are or how you came across the listing in the first place, they care about the profits and if you show them you can make a profit you will make a sale 99 times out of 100. What's more, in order to be a successful wholesaler, all you are ever going to need is one reliable buyer. Unless you are lucky enough to come across more good deals at a time than your buyer can handle, which is unlikely, the two of you can easily continue a profitable relationship for years.

Choosing the right property: In order to ensure that property wholesaling is worth your time, you will want to set a profit margin of at least $10,000 per property. While this might seem like a lot, it is important to keep in mind that these types of properties are not going to come along every day which means you need to work out to an average that makes it worth your while to keep searching for new leads each and every day. You are quite likely not going to have any luck with posted listings unless the property has returned to the market or has been listed for a prolonged period of time. Instead, you will want to consider the other options discussed in the proceeding chapters and try and catch people as early into the process of selling as possible for the best results.

When looking for properties, it is important to still have a fine line between potentially profitable and complete garbage. Remember, finding a cheap property in this instance is only going to be half of the battle, you are still going to need to find someone who is willing to take the property off your hands for somewhat more than you paid for it. To make this part of the process as easy as possible to will need to do everything you can to find properties that have ancillary benefits that make it clear that it will be worth the effort when someone else sees it for the first time.

This means you are going to want to look for properties in better neighborhoods, that, for one reason or another ended up going fallow. Likewise, the amenities in the area are often going to play a very important role as well. Additionally, you will want to keep in mind the target audience for the neighborhood that you are looking in and ensure it has things that appeal to them as well. The more airtight your case for why the property is worthwhile is, the easier it will be for you to successfully pass the property along to another investor.

Talking to the seller for the first time: The initial contact with the seller can easily go south if you make the mistake of not approaching them with confidence right off the bat. It is important to remember that by taking the property off their hands right away, with cash, you will likely be removing a large weight from their shoulders and allowing them to get on with whatever it is they will be doing now that the property is sold.

During this encounter, you will want to prepare a number of pre-scripted questions to ensure you gather all of the information you need while also gauging the motivation and integrity of the seller. You can ensure you come off confident to the seller by making sure you do as much homework as possible beforehand. Know the area that you are looking in as well as the cost of similar homes in the area and how this property is similar as well as different. The more knowledge you display off the bat, the more you will show them that you are a serious buyer and not someone who can be bargained with lightly.

A great way to go about showing that you know about the area, while still keeping the conversation casual is to ask how far the property is from a relevant local amenity such as a park or shopping center. Not only will this show that you know your stuff, it will help to build rapport with the seller as you are not just some outsider looking to take the property you are another member of the community.

While it might sound corny, the first few times you initially make contact with sellers, you should record the entire conversation and then listen back to it later, don't be afraid to take notes. Listening back to these conversations, later on, will help you to perfect your pitch and end up helping you turn a greater profit in the long run.

Offering the right price: After you have successfully found a property that could be worth wholesaling, and successfully made contact with the homeowner, the next thing you will need to do is take a look at the inside of the home and determine what the Maximum Allowed Offer (MAO) is going to be in order to ensure that you still end up turning a profit. This amount can be determined easily, all you will need to do is to ensure that the total value of the property, once it is ready to sell, is going to more than what you can realistically sell it to another person for after subtracting out the average 30 percent that property flippers like to take on new projects as well as what you hope you commission to be.

When you are first starting out you will likely need a little help in order to come up with the right numbers, but eventually, you will learn to determine specific repair costs in much the way that a contractor does, by breaking down the big job into individual tasks. To determine the expected ultimate selling value, you can look to what the current market average for homes of that size. With the right number in mind, you will then be ready to negotiate.

Negotiation: Perhaps more so than with any other type of real estate investment, those who practice property wholesaling, live and die based on their negotiation skills. Ideally, you will want to leave the other party feeling as though the deal that you came to was collaborative, even though it really benefits you far more than it benefits them.

When you go to present your primary offer, the first thing you will want to do is clearly lowball the owner as a means of ensuring that you have some room to make concessions moving forward. Right from the start, you are going to want to identify a few negotiation points that you can live without, along with those that you absolutely cannot and see how they can be traded accordingly. Additionally, you are going to want to strive to always do the negotiation face to face with the owner present as this puts you in a superior position of power. If it is currently a seller's market then you will want to hold the negotiation remotely if possible to negate the power advantage the seller would have during the negotiation.

Meeting the other party is also useful as it will allow you to more easily monitor their body language as a means of determining how the negotiation is going in real time. If a counteroffer is given along with open body language, for example, means that the other party is likely willing to compromise. If that same offer is given while the party is giving off standoffish body language then you know that they did not appreciate your first offer and are likely now responding in kind. If they express signs of being timid then you know that they are not confident in your counter offer which means you will likely see positive results if you attempt to lowball them even more.

Finally, if you are negotiating during a buyer's market then you will be able to make additional demands on the seller to go along with your offer and not have to worry about the deal falling through as a result. You will want to offer up a starting price that is 10 percent lower than would otherwise be the case and also ask that the owner's pay the closing costs on the deal. This part of the negotiation is crucial to ensuring that your meager profits don't have to go to paying for closing costs as well.

With that being said, it is important to not push the seller so far that they start to feel as though they can realistically find a better deal someplace else. While it is important to ensure that you get your price down to where you can make your desired finder's fee, it is equally not important to feel the need to squeeze every single penny out of the deal as possible. It will only take a single instance of this costing you a potentially profitable deal for all of that nickel and diming to end up being worth far less than the amount it ultimately ended up costing you. Don't forget, successfully wholesaling property is a marathon, not a sprint.

Making the most of the inspection period: The inspection period is the time after you have agreed to purchase a property that you have to do a final inspection to ensure that everything is in order before you officially pull the trigger. The inspection period is what makes it possible for property wholesaling in the first place as it gives you plenty of time to find an interested cash buyer as long as you move quickly. If you are planning on getting into the property wholesaler game it is best to have a few potential cash buyers lined up before you make any actual moves just to give yourself plenty of leeways in case things don't work out just how you planned.

However, you are fully able to take the risk of not finding a cash buyer in time as during that 14-day period you can call off the deal for practically any reason. The inspection period is your bubble of protection and it is best to make the most of it. While the inspection period has many benefits, that doesn't mean that you should neglect the initial reason for its existence. It is important to use the time to have an inspector come out and ensure that the property is actually up to snuff before it is too late to back out.

Chapter 5: Fix and Flip

If, when financing your first real estate investment, you found a partner who was willing to finance the full total of the operation then you are likely going to want to sell the property off as quickly as possible so that they can get their money and you can take your cut of the profits and use it to finance a real estate investment that is a little bit more lucrative. Unfortunately, standing between you and your ultimate payout is the myriad of things that can go wrong when it comes to fixing up a house in order to sell it for a profit.

Starting off on the right foot

ARV: When it comes to finding properties that will make the type of deal that fix and flip investors are looking for, it is all about the ARV or After the Retail Value. This is the amount that the property will ultimately be worth once it has been successfully renovated and brought to its peak state of perfection. When it comes to determining the ARV, you will always want to lowball it as overestimating can lead to a wide variety of potential issues while underestimating will only leave you with extra cash in your pocket.

To determine the ARV accurately, you will need to start with what you feel you will be able to purchase the property for and then add in the amount you expect the renovations will cost as well as any other fees or costs that might go in to completely taking control of the property. A standard ARV is going to leave about 30 percent room for profit, which means this is what your investor would be able to make if they facilitated the deal themselves. If you don't have the skills to do a realistic portion of the repairs yourself then you will need to ensure that whatever deal you offer your investor they have enough room to make 30 percent profit with room left over for you as well.

It is crucial to your long-term success in real estate investing that you determine the ARV for a property as quickly as possible and then stick to these investment rules as it will help prevent you from making poor decisions in the moment. While a 5 percent variance from your ARV might not sound like much, your margins are going to be slim enough as it is without changing things up on the fly.

Know the target audience: In order for the fix and flip process to proceed as smoothly as possible, the finished product needs to clearly appeal to a specific type of buyer. Knowing the target audience who will be ultimately buying the house makes it easier to know the true worth of the property and will also make the decisions required during renovation easier to come to. As a general rule, if you are looking to purchase in rural areas then you will want to prioritize properties with room for auxiliary vehicles or large animals along with any relevant zoning issues that may be required for such things. Alternately, if you are looking in a family friendly area then things like the quality of the local schools and extra bathrooms are going to be of utmost importance.

Take note of added value: While you are making improvements to the property, it is important to keep a running tally of all of the value that you ultimately add as you go along. Furthermore, you will want to ensure that the process is well documented to provide potential buyers will a clear idea of just how much work has gone into the renovations, thus helping to justify your current asking price.

This is not to say that you are going to want to take every project down to its frame and essentially start from scratch, far from it. Instead, you are only going to want to factor in the costs of potential changes that will cause the total value of the property to rise by at least 20 percent more than what you are going to make when it comes to additional profits. This means that you are generally going to need to think twice when it comes to projects such as enlarging a living room or remodeling a kitchen completely unless their current shape will make selling the property for a profit practically impossible. Keep in mind that the project is going to need to come in at or under budget in order for you to turn a profit which means the bottom line should always be at the forefront of all of your decisions.

When you eventually get to the point where you need to make a decision regarding things like decorating or painting it is crucial that you stick to neutral options in order to see the best results.

Not only are these options cheaper, they will make it easier for potential buyers to visualize their own stuff in the space. The one exception to this rule is flat white, it looks sterile and uninviting and is more likely to turn folks away from the home than anything else. First and foremost, you are going to want to ensure that you stick with choices that match the widest variety of color schemes possible. Each person who sees the property once it is finished should be able to automatically see themselves living there and an aggressive style or color choice is only going to appeal to a small portion of the population.

Keeping costs down

More so even than with traditional house flippers, you are going to want to do everything in your power in order to keep the cost of the renovation as low as possible. Doing so is going to require plenty of forethought and planning, as well as a strict dedication to the cause while the process is ongoing. Consider the following tips in order to remain as frugal as possible.

Take a micro view: One of the reasons that many new real estate investors have a hard time estimating out the cost of a remodel is that they try and determine the price they will have to pay as a whole rather than breaking everything down into its core components, adding together like products and then adding up the results. Not only will this process allow you to get a handle on just what all exactly needs to be done, it will save you money down the road when it comes time to purchase supplies.

Even better, it will give you a detailed breakdown to give to your investor to show them that you really have done your homework on the project.

When making this tally of tasks, you are going to want to go room by room through the property and write down each and everything that you will need to fix in order to get the room presentation ready. If you don't know how much something is likely to cost, it is much easier to find an estimate to fix a warped doorway than it is to put an entire broken house back together again. This list will ultimately also serve as a marketing tool as it will show potential sellers just how much work was done to get the house back into shape.

Cultivate suppliers: When you are pricing products you can also kill two birds with one stone by visiting local hardware stores and seeing what can be done about getting better prices in the long-term. Not only will solidifying these relationships save you money in both the short and long-term, having them in hand when you approach your investor about a project will give you more clout when it comes to proving your worth to the entire process.

In order to properly go about building these relationships, the first thing you need to understand is that bulk orders like yours can represent a serious windfall to a smaller store, which is why they will likely be more susceptible to your pitch. Before you go in, add up the total cost of your potential purpose and lead with this number. Explain to them what you are looking for and that you are hoping to build a long-term relationship with as few suppliers as possible. While not every store is going to be agreeable to your proposition, it likely won't take more than a few stops for someone to be willing to give you a discount. With that number in hand, you can then move on to other business and use the discount you have already obtained to get an even better discount elsewhere. Discounts of 20 percent or more are not unheard of, and as buying last minute supplies is one of the biggest drains on the most fix and flip projects, this 20 percent can be a huge help.

Know how to find the right deals: Besides buying in bulk, you will also want to develop the habit of always being on the lookout for good deals. While it won't make sense to buy every product before you even know you need it, there are a surprising number of evergreen products that you can pick up for a fraction of their normal price if you keep an eye out for the right sales. Then, when you approach your investor with a new project, you have more than just a good deal to show them, you have actual skin in the game when it comes to collateral. A good example of this type of preparation is granite countertops. Nothing easily classes up a bathroom like granite countertops and if you know how to find it, you can get it for pennies on the dollar. The secret is to find a granite that has flaws in the center and then cut them out yourself when fitting them to the sink.

Find the right crew

While being handy and able to handle some portion of the work on the property yourself will make it much easier to get an investor to go along with your plans, it is practically impossible to complete a fix and flip in a reasonable timeframe without help. This means you are going to need to assemble a team you can count on and have them ready to go when you take your project to your investor. Like having materials on hand and knowing the right distributors, having a team on hand makes you more valuable in the equation than you otherwise would be.

While a good team is always going to cost money, if you take your time and source your members carefully, you should be able to organize one that is willing to wait for payment until the job is done. While this will likely require more effort on your part than if you are able to put some money down up front, the end result will be a team that you can count on to have your back throughout the renovation process. While hiring the best possible options will likely end up cutting into your overall profits, the fix and flip strategy is all about quantity of quality. Having the best team around will allow you to complete more jobs in a shorter period of time which will ultimately end up generating a greater amount of revenue than squeezing every possible penny out of every single project.

Legal team: The first two people that you are going to want on your team are a good real estate lawyer and a certified public account who is familiar with real estate regulations. Both of these individuals will likely be willing to answer many of the questions you have at this point as part of a free consultation, and if you explain your situation they will likely be willing to bill you at a future point for any paid services you might require for the time being. While the fees you will have to pay eventually won't be cheap, having these folks in your corner could easily make the difference between success and failure if you find yourself suddenly in need of their services in a bad way.

Agent: Unless you are only planning to flip a few houses, it is important that you take the time to find a real estate agent that you can build a long-term relationship with. Not only will this make it easier to ultimately sell the properties that you do find, it will also potentially give you access to deals that you might not hear about otherwise. Have this aspect of the process already sewn up will make the latter parts of the process much easier which means you can move on to your next money-making venture as quickly as possible.

Contractor: Finally, finding the right contractor for the job is crucial to ensuring that you end up making money off of your investment property. The contractor will be in charge of the entire operation and will ideally come with their own crew which means you won't need to worry about hiring a wide variety of different specialists and can instead focus on hiring a single person you can really trust. A quality contractor can easily be the difference between success and failure for any one of a hundred reasons.

As such, it is important to try and get a referral for a quality contractor if possible. If you don't have a real estate investment club to turn to for advice, tracking down a local real estate inspector is also a good choice as they will likely remember the names of the contractors whose work they most respect. As an added bonus, building up a good relationship with a real estate inspector is likely to pay off in the future as well. If this doesn't work you can try visiting lumber mills and asking about contractors who always purchase the highest quality materials. This level of dedication will likely carry over into other aspects of their job as well.

Once you have the list of potential candidates in hand, the first thing you are going to want to do is a phone interview so you don't waste too much time on the options that you don't connect with. You will want to touch on things like their previous experience, the number of jobs they work on simultaneously (the fewer the better), what their team is like and references.

After the phone interviews narrow the field you will then want to have a face to face interview to ensure that you and the contractor get along well and can stand to be around one another for more than 20 minutes at a stretch. If everything goes well, you will likely be spending quite a bit of time with this person, it is important that you get along with them. Meeting in person will also allow you to explain exactly what you are looking for and verify that they will be willing to wait for payment until after the property has sold. You are going to want a contractor and a backup contractor ready to go before moving forward with the buying process.

Chapter 6: Rent to Own Rental Properties

In most cases, when it comes to buying a home, an offer is placed on the property and then it is collected upon at the time that ownership is transferred. While this typically results in a mortgage for the purchaser, an alternative known as a lease option or a lease-to-own option is an alternative that can allow you to get your hands on some property without any of the traditional hassles.

Rent to own agreements are going to vary by state as many states are going to have different regulations regarding the specifics. The time frame for these types of agreements is typically going to be anywhere between 1 and 3 years, after which the opportunity to purchase the property becomes available. It won't be as simple as just paying the rent for three years and then getting your name on the title, there are other conditions that will need to be met as well.

The initial amount that will need to be put down at the time the property is rented (that will be paid by your eventual renters) is known as option money. This will ideally give you the right, not the obligation, to purchase the property at the time in question if you so desire. If you sign a lease-purchase, not a lease-option, then you are going to be required to buy the property after the lease expires.

The contract will also specify how the price of the property will be determined when the time comes to purchase. The value may be based on what the property was worth at the time the contract was signed, or it can be reevaluated at the time the lease comes up for an option. Ideally, you will want to lock the price in when the contract is signed as odds are not in you favor that the property will be worth less in the future.

During the lease period, the buyer will pay the seller rent as normal (which will be paid by another renter) a portion of each rent payment will be used for what is known as rent credit. This credit is applied to the ultimate purchase price of the property and is deducted from what needs to be paid once the option is available.

When determining the contract, it is important to keep an eye out for additional fees such as property taxes and homeowner association fees as you will need to factor these into the price you charge for rent on the property as well. Even if the seller is currently covering these fees it is important to take out a rental insurance policy and add it to the cost of the rent. It is only about $30 a month in most cases and can even be a selling point in your listing. It is very important to be crystal clear on what is covered under maintenance fees as lawn or pool care is very different from replacing a malfunctioning air conditioner. Finally, it is important that you include a clause saying that you don't need to make the initial payment for a few weeks or more. This will give you the ability to find renters to take your place

Finding a tenant

Once you have convinced your new landlord to rent you the property in a few weeks or more, all you need to do is get the money together to complete the transaction within that time. To do so, you are going to want to post the property to as many different rental websites as possible and look for interested parties who are going to be moving into the area from out of town. A deposit to hold the property until they can make it into town is enough to get the property into your name and you are then on hand to provide them with the keys when they arrive.

In order to attract the right types of tenants, the first thing you are going to need to do is to ensure that you price the rental property so that in three years you end up with enough of a profit in order to convert the rent to own agreement into a more traditional mortgage. This will likely drop the amount required to pay for the property significantly each month, which will then allow you to see additional profits on top of allowing the renters to pay for the property in its entirety.

In order to ensure that you can turn a profit on the property that you are going to be renting out, while also guaranteeing that you can rent it out in the time you have available, the first thing you are going to need to do is to determine the tier of the property. The first tier is comprised of high-quality properties in the best neighborhoods and is sure to never stay empty for long. These types of properties often have unique amenities in the area or on the property which you can use as a major selling point when you are relisting the property. Tier two properties are still quite nice, though the neighborhood is going to be a little older and there will be fewer obvious unique amenities. You can typically still work with these types of properties but it might be a little close when it comes down to whether or not you can seal the deal. Lower tiers of property often stay on the market for much longer periods of time and it is unlikely they will work out in your compacted timeframe.

When it comes to marketing your future rental successfully, the first thing you are going to need to keep in mind is that everyone is only two points of social connection from someone who is either about to move or is thinking about an upcoming move. With odds like that, the most profitable place to let the world know about your rental property is on social media. Your perfect tenant is only a few shares away.

When it comes to choosing the right tenant, it is important to do your homework and assure that they can pay the rent on time and don't have a history with the types of crime that could end up getting your property seized as a crime scene. Time is of the essence, however, which is why you may want to excuse the occasional legal slip up as long as they don't have a history of evictions and their credit report comes back clean. If you do go through the application process and deny the applicant, be aware that you are legally required to send them a letter explaining why they were not chosen.

Outlining a lease

Once you have found a tenant that fits your qualifications, the final step standing between you and making a reliable return on your investment is a lease that clearly outlines your expectations in such a way that leaves you confident the tenant won't be able to do something potentially dangerous or destructive. While a good lease is always important to a landlord, as the property isn't yours yet, it is especially important in this instance that everything is ironclad or the whole plan can easily fall apart. When it comes to an effective lease agreement the first thing you will want to do is to make it clear just what your expectations are in regard to every part of the property.

It doesn't matter how obvious you think a certain action or behavior is to do or not do if you don't put it in the lease agreement you can practically guarantee a tenant will try and do or not do it. In addition, making it clear upfront what is expected from the tenant is a fair way to ensure that everyone is on the same page when it comes to expectations. Tenants are more likely to follow the rules that you have set forth if they are clearly explained up front and in writing, this way it is clear that they understand what the results of breaking those rules would ultimately be.

Most importantly perhaps, having a clear list of rules and consequences for breaking those rules in place at the start of the landlord and renter relationship will make it much easier for you to take legal action to remove the tenant if needed. To wit, here are a few rules that every landlord should consider, feel free to add your own as needed:

How late rent will be handled: Even the best tenant has a bad day, which is why the first thing you will want to include on your agenda is to determine the date each month that rent needs to be paid by, if the tenant has any wiggle room in regards to late rent (a day is perfectly acceptable) as well as an option to discuss alternative scenarios if presented in advance, again, everyone has a bad day and being seen as a nice landlord will have its advantages as well.

When it comes to determining penalty fees, there are multiple options. First, you can charge a flat fee based on the lateness in question, a percentage of the total or simply a fixed dollar amount. While you are largely left to your own devices, in this case, it is important to be familiar with local laws and ordinances to ensure you do not overstep your bounds. Again, it is important to set an amount that is strict enough to be seen as a penalty without being needlessly harsh. The benefits you will reap by being seen as a benevolent landlord will extend to naturally prompt payment and an overall improved level of care being extended to the property.

How and when you can enter the property: This is another point that is extremely important to clearly elucidate to your tenant in case the time comes where you do need to enter the property. Typically, this can only occur with a justifiable cause and with a previous warning. Again, it is important to determine the rules in your state to ensure you are not overstepping your boundaries while also preventing yourself from giving up unnecessary freedoms. Whatever you decide, it is important it is clear and well explained to prevent any misunderstandings at a later point. There are few things that can cause renters to react poorly than an unexpected visit from you, especially if you thought you already made it clear you were coming.

How garbage will be handled: While this is certainly one of those instances where it would seem that certain levels of decorum would go without saying, in reality, if the issue is not made clear upfront, garbage can be a contentious issue between landlords and tenants. This isn't just a cleanliness issue or one that relates to how your property is being treated, you can literally find yourself in legal trouble if a property you own is full of garbage, even if you do not currently live there.

As such it is important to make it clear to the tenant that regular garbage removal is to be expected as well as the rules and regulations for recycling. You also need to make it clear that clutter of any type, including vehicles, cannot stay in the yard or on the property for more than a short period of time. You should still include a clause that makes the tenant responsible for fees related to garbage removal, just in case.

Make it clear what level of upkeep is expected: It is important to outline the acceptable level of care that is required when it comes to keeping the outside of the home in a presentable shape. It is typically a good idea to keep the landscaping requirements to a minimum as that will make it more likely they are actually being followed. Landscaping costs can quickly get out of hand, so if there is a substantial amount of upkeep required, clearly outline who is in charge of doing what.

Outline the fact that the tenant needs to respect their neighbors: Again, this seems like an obvious one, but it is important to make it clear that any period after 9 pm or 10 pm and before 8 am should be considered quiet time out of respect for the neighbors. While this might not be strictly necessary, your neighbors will certainly thank you for it in the long run.

Cover your appliances: The appliances in the kitchen are likely the most expensive individual items in the entire house. As such, you should definitely include a clause that indicates the appropriate use for each item and the fact that the tenant will pay for any repair to these items for uses that are deemed by you to be outside of their intended specifications. This should include things like what is acceptable to be put into the garbage disposal as well as general hygiene tips like cleaning the refrigerator on a regular basis. Remember, it is better to be safe than sorry, take the time to cover your bases and eventually, you will almost certainly be glad you did.

How do you feel about pets: Your policy regarding pets is almost entirely up to you, though it is best to have one of some sort that is clearly outlined to prevent large or violent animals from taking up residence. Regardless of what you chose, there will be people who are interested in renting the property. It is important to keep in mind, however, that you can always allow pets at a later date, you can't ever return the property to a pet free state.

Regardless of the rules, you decide to set down in advance, it is important to always check and make sure you are following your rights as a landlord and not overstepping your authority. It is important to set reasonable response to repeated transgressions, and to above all, follow through on anything you put into writing. If your tenant observes an unchecked breach of the stated rules, the overall quality of their behavior will go down nearly 100 percent of the time. Try and be fair, but firm, for the longest lasting results.

Conclusion

Thank you for making it through to the end of *Investing in Real Estate: How to Get into the Real Estate Game with NO MONEY DOWN*, let's hope it was informative and able to provide you with all of the tools you need to achieve your goals, whatever it is that they may be. Just because you've finished this book doesn't mean there is nothing left to learn on the topic, expanding your horizons is the only way to find the mastery you seek.

The next step is to stop reading already and to get ready to pound the pavement on the lookout for good deals and for the people that will help make your goal a reality. When you are first starting out it is important to do so with the right expectations to ensure that you don't burn out before you start to see results. This means understanding that what you are trying to do is one of the most difficult types of real estate investment to pull off, especially for a beginner. Practically, what this means is that you are going to end up hearing no far more often than you ever end up hearing yes. When faced with the seemingly endless number of negative responses, remember that all you are going to need is one yes to make it all worth it.

The good news is that the first time is going to be the most difficult because you have few of the tools and contacts you need to make your dream a reality. This won't be the case with future projects, however, so it may help your morale to keep in mind that the initially endless legwork will only have to be done once, next time you will be able to jump right to asking your contacts if they are interested in another profitable project.

Finally, if you found this book useful in any way, a review on Amazon is always appreciated!

Description

Investing in real estate is one of the easiest ways to generate a reliable passive income in the long-term. Despite this well-known fact, there are millions of people out there with the credit and the skills to profit from the real estate market just sitting on their hands as they feel they don't have perhaps the most important thing of all in order to get started. Finding the capital to make their first real estate investment is the number one reason that most people don't fulfill their real estate potential. While not without its difficulties, finding complete funding for a project is far from insurmountable and *Investing in Real Estate: How to Get into the Real Estate Game with NO MONEY DOWN* can teach you everything you need to know in order to turn your real estate dreams into reality.

Inside you will learn everything you need to know in order to rig the system to ensure that you can profit from a successful real estate investment, despite the fact that you didn't actually put so much as one penny down to cover any of the costs. While this might sound far-fetched, the truth of the matter is that professional real estate investors do it every day through a process of maximizing their borrowing position, presenting the best deals to lends and knowing where money is.

What's more, you will also find everything you need to know in order to get started in not just one but with three different distinct real estate investing plans, each of which is designed to ensure you turn a profit without opening your own purse strings even a fraction of an inch. So, what are you waiting for? Say goodbye to your boring old 9-to-5 job and start planning for your independently wealthy future, buy this book today!

Inside you will find

- Easy ways to use the laws to your advantage and ensure your credit report is as squeaky clean as possible.
- How a direct mailing campaign can lead to a wealth of viable real estate investments that are 100 percent free of competition or real estate agent interference.
- The multitude of ways you can use foreclosed properties to turn a profit.
- Each and every type of potential private lender and how to best get on their good sides.
- A surefire way to get the money for your deal within 24-hours, assuming you have a deal that is worth the excitement.
- The secret to making money on real estate investments despite owning a property for less than two weeks and making no renovations.
- Easy ways to make yourself as attractive to hard money lenders as possible.
- Top options when it comes to crowdfunding your next real estate investment.
- ***And more…***

www.ingramcontent.com/pod-product-compliance
Lightning Source LLC
Chambersburg PA
CBHW050016230526
45470CB00003B/994